Contents

Welcome! 3

Unit 1: My Garden 7

Unit 2: My School 12

Unit 3: At the Farm 17

Unit 4: At Home 22

Unit 5: My Day 27

Unit 6: At the Beach 32

Unit 7: A Day Out 37

Unit 8: Animals 42

Certificate 47

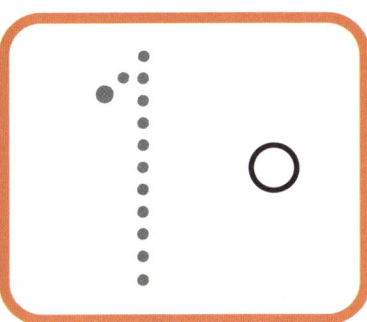

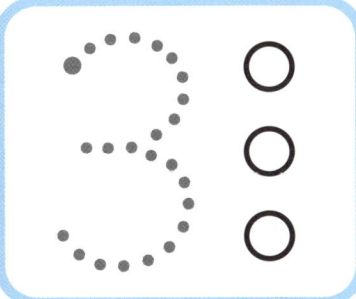

Welcome Unit, Lesson 3: Chant

Track 8

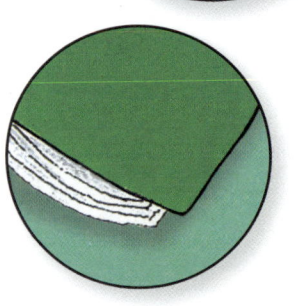

Welcome Unit, Lesson 4: Vocabulary

Track 9

Track 10

My Garden

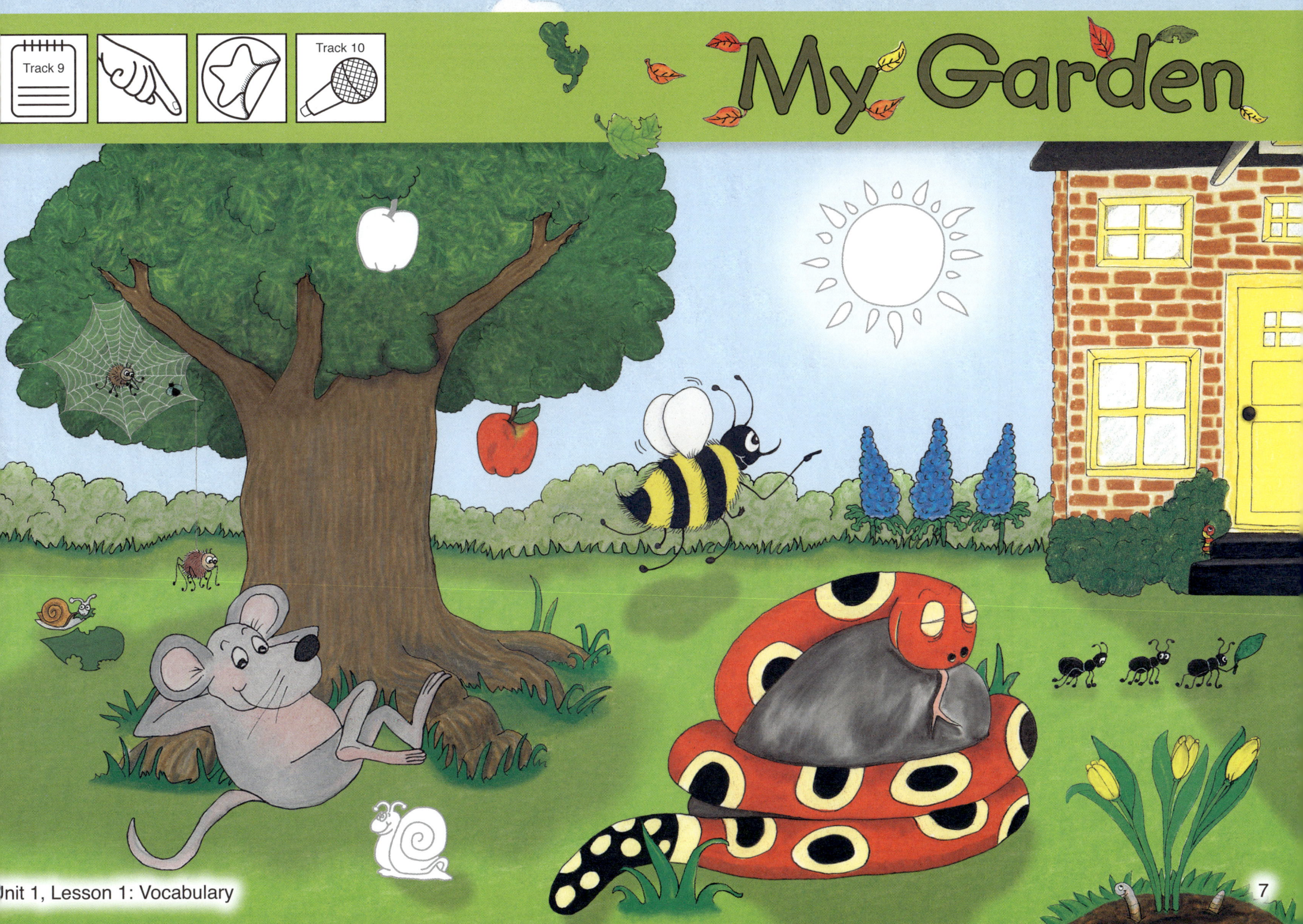

Unit 1, Lesson 1: Vocabulary

7

Unit 1, Lesson 2: Vocabular

Track 13

Unit 1, Lesson 3: Story

Review 1: /s/, /a/, /t/

My School

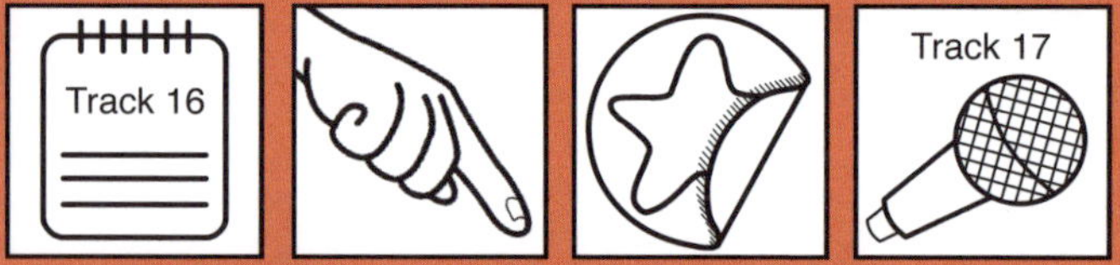

Unit 2, Lesson 1: Vocabulary

Unit 2, Lesson 2: Vocabulary

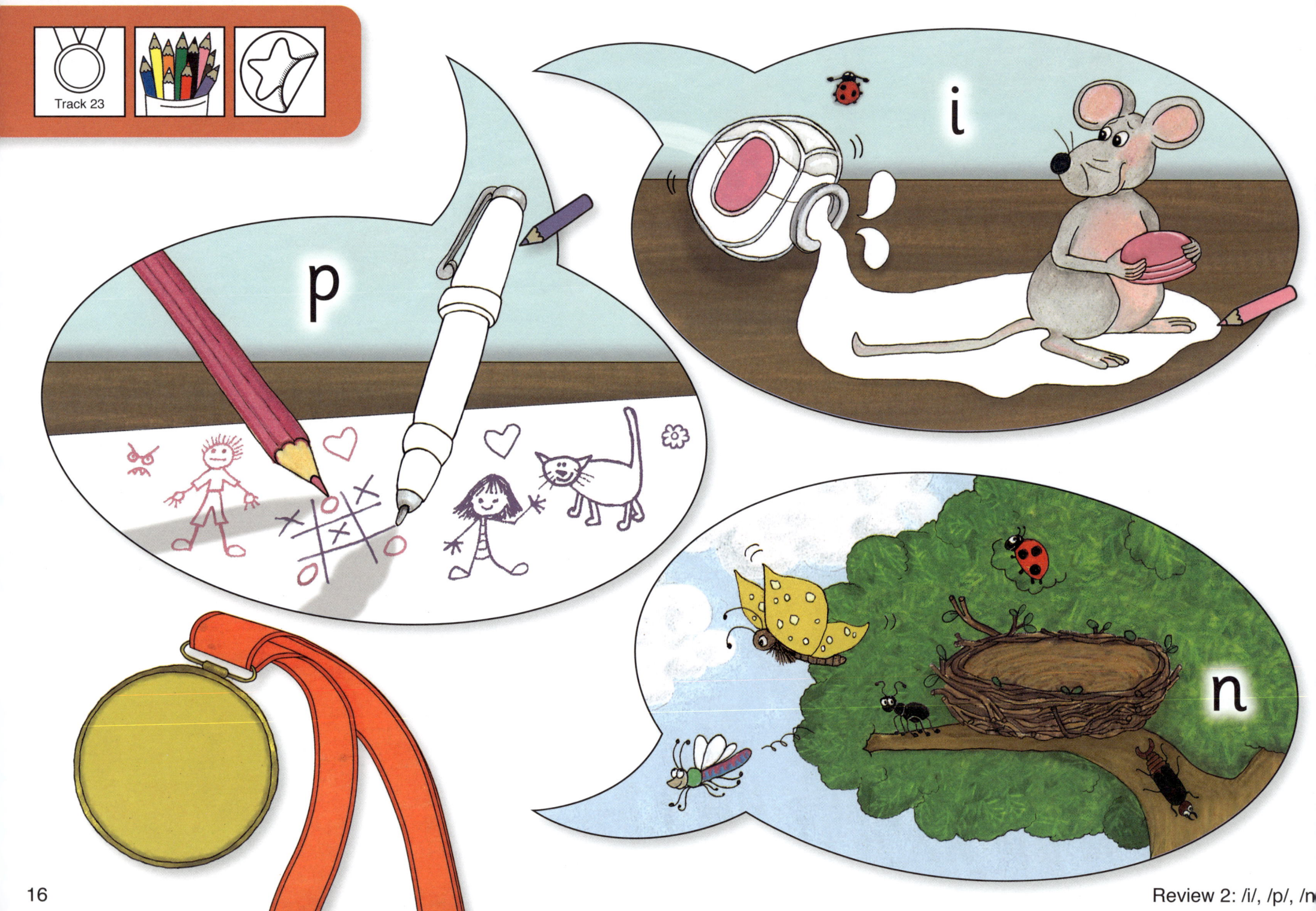

Track 27

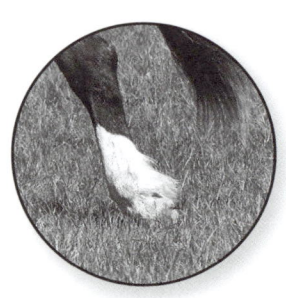

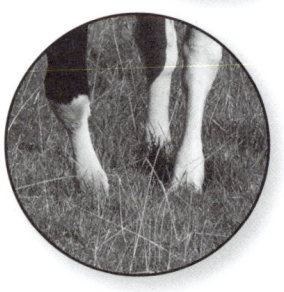

18

Unit 3, Lesson 2: Vocabulary

Track 28

Unit 3, Lesson 3: Story

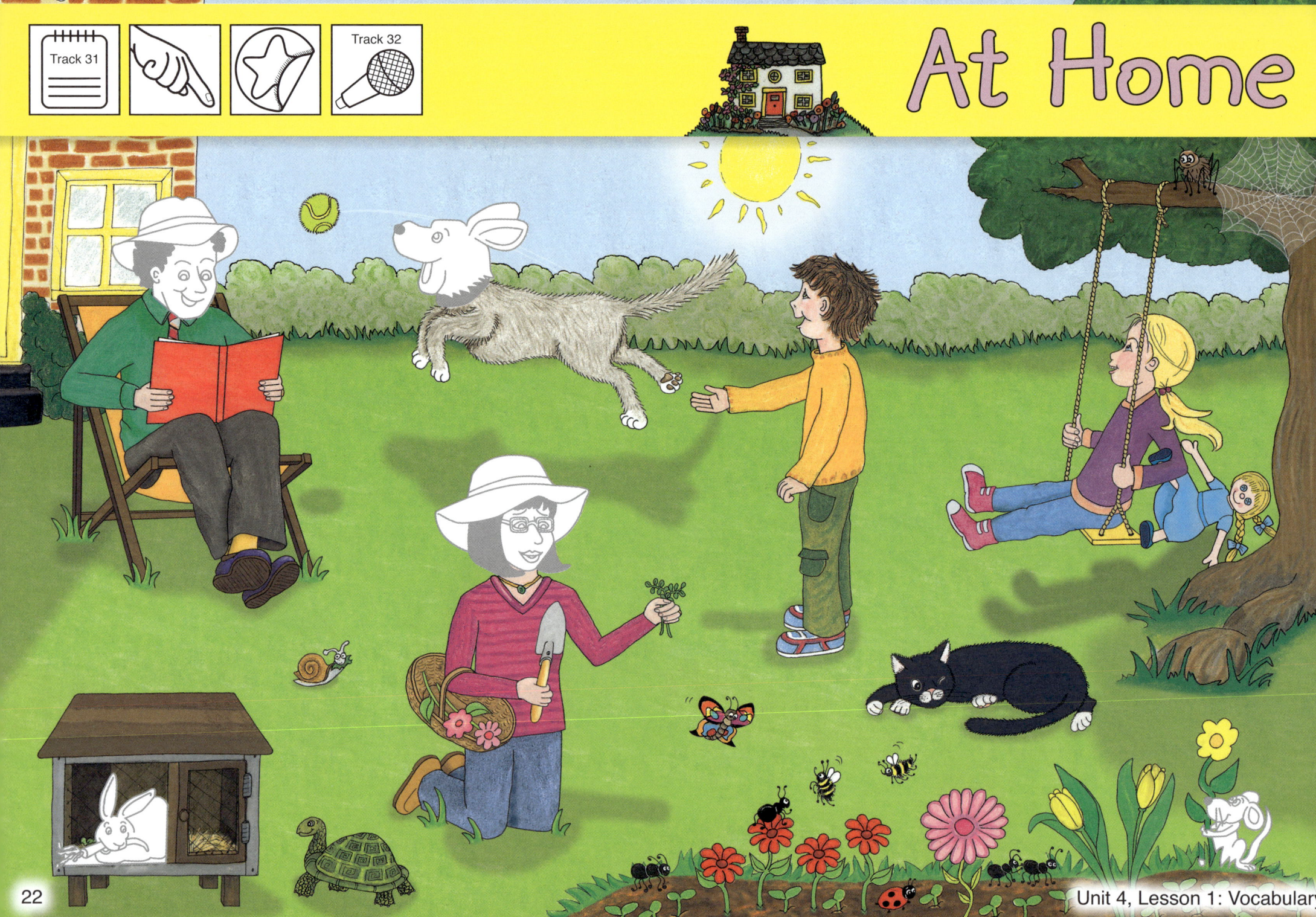

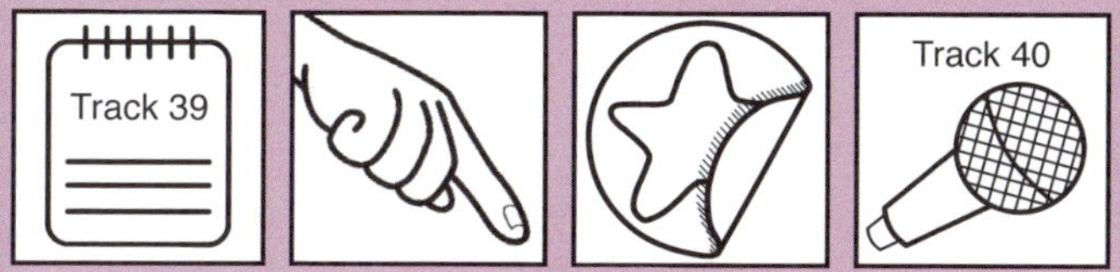

 Track 39    Track 40

 My Day

Unit 5, Lesson 1: Vocabulary

At the Beach

Track 50

Unit 6, Lesson 3: Story

Review 6: /f/, /b/, /a

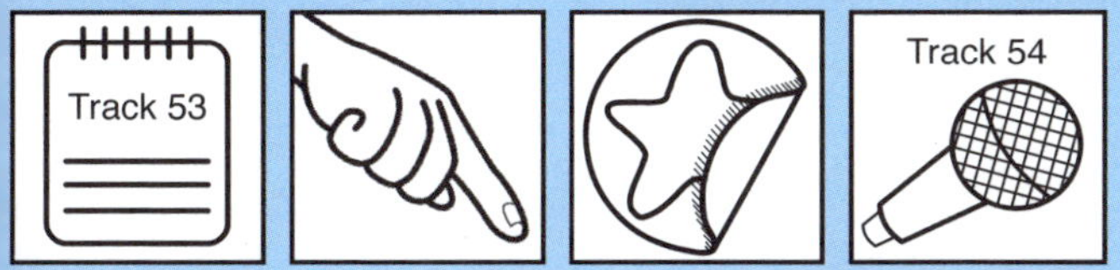

A Day Out

Unit 7, Lesson 1: Vocabulary

Unit 7, Lesson 2: Vocabulary

 Track 61    Track 62

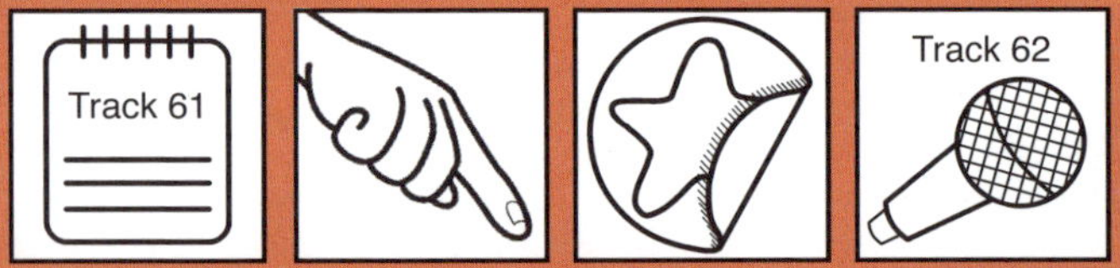

 Animals

Unit 8, Lesson 1: Vocabulary

Unit 8, Lesson 2: Vocabulary

Track 67

Unit 8, Lesson 4: Song